ERIC BURDON:
REBEL WITHOUT A PA

PHILIP J. PAYNE

© Marianna Burdon

New Bridge Publications

This book could not have been created without the help and support of the following:

Eric Burdon for his cooperation and support.
Marianna Burdon for her photographic contribution.
David Brown for his creative collaboration.
John Steel & Kathy Etchingham for their prompting of memories.

And my wife, Carol, for her patience and guidance.

ISBN: 9780993195600

Photos: Newcastle Libraries, Philip J. Payne, Marianna Burdon, Jimmy Perry.
Cover image: Bill Orchard/Rex Shutterstock
Design: David Hepworth

Published by:
Newcastle Libraries
New Bridge Publications, 2015
www.tynebridgepublishing.co.uk

ERIC BURDON: REBEL WITHOUT A PAUSE

PHILIP J. PAYNE

This is a slice of Eric Burdon's life from my perspective, from when we were growing up, to how I know him now. The following is not meant to be a 'man behind the music' account or an attempt to chronicle the vast compendium of music, recordings and discography produced over the last fifty-plus years of his musical output and colourful career. It is a description of a friend from my youth, right up to today. He survived being born in a poor part of the UK during World War Two, endured post war deprivation, a poor education, bullying, an inherited health issue and short stature (which was made up for by huge endowment elsewhere). Despite all this he became 'Rock & Roll Hall of Fame' famous and rich, and yet at the end of every phone call, even today, never fails to say 'give me luv t' the missus.'

Rebel Without a Pause author Philip J. Payne with Eric Burdon in 'The Shark'

TYNESIDE

Tyneside was tough all over, but toughest of all was Walker, Eric's childhood home and the beating heart of shipbuilding Tyneside. Its masculine culture exalted the virtues of skill, pride, workmanship, dependability, fraternal loyalty, team spirit and fortitude – all critical to its dangerous seafaring, shipbuilding and coal-mining occupations. The same culture would condone gambling away a whole week's pay packet or drinking ten pints of beer and getting into a fist fight before heading for home on a Friday night.

In his favour, Eric was an in-the-bone Geordie, as Tynesiders are known, with local hero, Geordie Ridley in his ancestry. Geordie Ridley was the celebrated music hall artist, writer and composer of the Tyneside anthem, *Blaydon Races*. Ridley trusted those around him, who then took advantage and took his cash. (Ridley felt swindled out of the proceeds of *Blaydon Races* and perhaps history repeated itself when The Animals disagreed about their financial arrangements).

Some of the antics of Geordie lads in the name of machismo might help to explain the attitude that Eric brought with him to rock stardom. For example, just for the sheer balls of it, defying the management's dire warnings, shipyard apprentices at Walker would run and leap into the uncovered openings left in the decks of the cavernous hulls of the big tankers during construction. There were safety nets strung across the void some 20 feet below the deck level, but even so…

BORN ON TYNESIDE: WHERE MEN BUILT SUPERTANKERS AT ONE END OF THE STREET AND DRANK ENOUGH TO FLOAT THEM AT THE OTHER. DAVID BROWN

View of the industrial Tyne from North Shields, 1960s.

Geordies walking to work along Welbeck Road, Walker (Eric's home town and suburb of Newcastle), 18 June 1901.

THE BURDON OF THE ENGLISH

It can be argued that Eric Victor Burdon was the 'greatest singer of the 1960s British blues explosion bar none,' said Anthony de Curtis of *Rolling Stone*. David Bowie once said, 'sometimes it's better not to meet your idols, that way they stay intact.' I can verify Eric Burdon is totally intact. At seventy-four, he is as alert, inquisitive, creative, argumentative and as stubborn as he ever was. He is also totally uncompromising. This, perhaps genetically inbuilt, trait has also caused him to have many difficult times throughout his career.

Eric is still a stone cold Geordie. Geordies are just a little bit different. They can be permanently defensive, talking and behaving as if they personally own the ground they stand on and they are famous for speaking their minds. These traits and his inbuilt inability to take the middle of the road, have brought Eric a lot of problems during his career, but they are also the secret of his success. If *he's* doing it – a major gig or making scrambled eggs – he'll do it his way or it won't be done at all.

The English in general are introspective and downbeat about themselves, but not Geordies. Justified or not, Geordies believe they have their own, unique place in the universe and they can do anything they put their minds to.

The English can be a bewildering people, the stereotypes are well known; lost an empire – failed to find another role, an island mentality with teeth-grinding superiority, stubborn class divisions and a pervading sense of failure. This is what the English say about themselves, except for Geordies, they are tough buggers.

In his time, Eric Burdon has delivered or interpreted just about every music genre there is except Gregorian chants, but knowing Eric even that's still possible. Eric, with his unwavering belief in himself, has risen again and again like the proverbial Phoenix from the ashes of broken marriages, drug busts, cancelled concerts, inadvisable public outbursts, jail time, broken limbs, shameful managers, manipulative record companies and the implosion of what was potentially a historic band (in fact Eric told me The Animals could have eventually morphed into punk which was perfectly fine with him, but the other members of the band were too reticent. A 'protopunk' scene was indeed already emerging in the early sixties in England.)

Yet, somehow he always manages to rise from the chaos – he's always in the entertainment news, he's going into movies, he's writing a book, he's going solo, he's putting a new band together. There's never a dull moment around Eric.

Music critic Keith Altham once said of Eric, 'always a trier, always a dreamer, always a brave heart – if sometimes a tad wrong-headed.' Keith might be describing Don Quixote.

Quayside, Newcastle, 1960. (TWAM)

EVOLVING ANIMALS

was fortunate enough to see the first seeds emerge of hat became The Animals; there could not have been a more unlikely or disparate group of people. As an individual, Eric has always been solid blues all the way. Drummer, John Steel was firmly a jazz enthusiast. Bass guitarist, Chas Chandler loved the pop scene and the Beatles. Keyboardist, Alan Price had ambitions of writing musicals and lead guitarist, Hilton Valentine, man did he love skiffle!

Add to this unlikely collaboration of characters the fact that most of the music they played and subsequently became famous for, was inspired by old, poor, black American men that were virtually unheard of in England at the time. In fact, it was very rare to see anyone outside of London in the fifties who wasn't snow white, particularly in the North East of England where in those days 'mixed marriages' were frowned upon – by mixed, they meant between Catholics and Protestants. The only black men we Geordies saw as kids were coalminers, covered in coal dust.

The band pulled off quite a feat despite internal discord, there were not many instances when they were all on the same page at the same time. Eric sometimes refers to The Animals in those days as being a 'no' band because of the constant disagreements. Celebrity PR man Keith Altham said '*Spinal Tap* had nothing on The Animals'.

The Animals, early 60s. (Dezo Hoffmann/Rex Shutterstock)

IT'S HIS LIFE (AND HE'LL DO WHAT HE WANTS)

The familiar voice on the phone said 'I just realised man (*Man* – Geordie for male friend, not the hippy 'Maaan'), I don't have a good drug story for this book.' This might seem strange to some who know Eric's familiarity with mind altering substances, but his statement actually didn't faze me.

What he meant was he did not have a story about heroin, crack or meth for his new book. One secret to his longevity is he never got into those drugs in a serious way. Pot, LSD and other psychedelic and hallucinatory recreational products were not *real* drugs in his mind.

One morning, on a recent stayover at Eric's I had already been up for a couple of hours. Eric's wife, Marianna was out of town, Eric still in bed. Eric likes to cook breakfast, but I was hungry so I scrounged around for something to eat until he got up. I took a plastic bag of ginger snaps out of the fridge and sat down in the dining room to read. I was sinking my fangs into cookie number three when Eric came ambling around the corner from the kitchen, as soon as he saw me he rushed at me shouting 'no, no, no!' and waving his arms. It seems I was eating his 'special' cookies, I thought they were a bit bland for ginger snaps. Funny thing is, they didn't affect me at all.

For the last nine months, we have been going over, sorting out and adding to the handwritten and typed contents for Eric's new book at his house in Ojai, California. There were already pages and pages of drug-fuelled anecdotes and wild adventures. The pages were laid out in rows along the kitchen counter and streaming into the living room.

My role was mostly as a date and fact checker, the latter being the more difficult of the two. Previously published discographies and release dates help a lot to verify events. As to the facts, well Eric describes all of his experiences, some are real, some are perhaps hallucinatory, but to him they are all real events and he tells his stories exactly how remembers them.

Animals' drummer John Steel had a slightly differen[t] take on Eric's two previous autobiographies when h[e] told me 'Well, he's a really canny lad (a Geordi[e] expression which means *nice*), but I just can['t] understand why he makes so much stuff up. He's ha[d] an interesting life, why over-egg the pudding?' I don['t] think John's comment was quite right, but I understoo[d] his perspective. We all see and remember the sam[e] things differently. Eric's anecdotes are all about rea[l] people and events, perhaps heavily garnished wit[h] Burdon wit and imagination. Yes, they might sometime[s] be embellished, out of almost all recognition, until th[e] incidents he recounts bear only the slendere[st] resemblance to the original experience.

Eric is a remarkably prolific story teller with anothe[r] Tyneside trait, he tells it all, even if it makes him loo[k] like a jerk. While he is a great story teller he is also a[n] avid reader and movie enthusiast, he has an extensiv[e] library of books and DVDs that spills into every area o[f] the house.

While we are working during the day the backgroun[d] music will come from the well-stocked, vintage 1970[s] juke box in his living room, it plays an eclectic mix o[f] artists ranging from Tom Jones and Amy Winehouse t[o] Creedence Clearwater, Chuck Berry, Bo Diddley and Jo[e] Turner as well as original Animals and Eric Burdon [&] War numbers. This is a large comfortable room with [a] big leather sofa and Klipsch 600W tower-speakers o[n] either side of the fireplace. On top of one of the tower[s] is displayed his black nickel 'Rock & Roll Hall of Fam[e] statuette.

Today, at seventy-four, Eric is still a super-absorben[t] sponge of information of all kinds. Forever linked to Th[e] Animals, sometimes by choice and sometimes not, he i[s] very much his own man; even with his strong sense o[f] identity he has sometimes found it hard to protect hi[s] own interests. His surroundings, his relationships, hi[s] career and life experiences are expressed in his musi[c] and song writing. He is an 'idea a minute' man, pickin[g]

A cafe near Ojai, Eric's 1971 Chevy Impala, known as 'The Shark' in the background.

up inspiration from everywhere and everything, he is a constant verbal stream of ideas, thoughts and reflections. Whether it's driving, walking at the beach or in the mountains, or just lying in the backyard he sucks it all in and ideas come spewing out.

Even with all this, I feel that he has never given himself enough credit for the contributions he has made to rock music history; he is pretty self-effacing (for a Geordie). In a way, he has had multiple careers in the music industry, he is also several 'Eric Burdons' and can turn his focus on and off like a switch. He has a profound social consciousness, is generous to a fault, irritating, obstinate, uncompromising and still manages to challenge the status quo.

Another key to his survival is that he knew his goal from the beginning. He told me 'I knew right from the start that I would never be a number one solo artist, but I knew I could make a mark in the music world.' With that philosophy he avoided overreaching, burning out early and joining the 'Twenty-Seven Forever Club'. Eric is an intense, slow burn and talking with him on one subject will spawn ten more.

"ERIC IS A DESERT DENIZEN THROUGH AND THROUGH. BORN IN WALKER, NEWCASTLE HE NOW LIVES IN OJAI, CALIFORNIA."

For me, working with Eric is very easy as we have identical likes and dislikes of entertainment, philosophies and social issues. We have the same taste in music. We are both movie fans and love absurd and surrealistic comedy. We have always been pegged as inveterate practical jokers, although Eric was always way ahead of me. He told me that one time on tour when Hilton Valentine was asleep, he put Hilton's hands in a bowl of water and for a moment on waking Hilton thought he had peed himself.

There is no doubt Eric has led one hell of an interesting life. His house is full of his writing, lyrics, poetry, drawings and sketches. He is like a tap that can't turn off. Despite all the setbacks during his life – his house burning down, family problems, the sometimes acrimonious disputes with record companies, missing out on the *The House of the Rising Sun* royalties and losing the right to use The Animals' name (the band name that he proposed and certainly has been synonymous with for the last 50 years), he is remarkably pragmatic.

While surprisingly philosophical about all the setbacks and disappointments, one can sense there are still some exposed nerve endings, usually when the name Alan Price surfaces, but he is determined to stay his own course, put the past behind him and is resolute in the belief he has a lot more to get out there yet. His voice is still phenomenal as can be heard on his latest album '*Til Your River Runs Dry*. How does that voice come out of someone who has had asthma attacks since childhood? This long-term asthmatic condition has been severely debilitating at times but he has never let it interfere with his live performances

For all the ups and downs of his career, Eric is far less touchy now than when I got to know him in art college in the fifties. He has always had to fight hard and sometimes it's hard to stop fighting even when the battle is won. In his business the battle is never really over, and it seems the more famous you become, the more precarious your position is.

Eric was both pleased and surprised that Bruce Springsteen had tweeted him while they were both at SXSW in Austin, Texas and asked Eric to join him o stage. It was a sort of validation for Eric in a way, at thi time in life we all need to feel we are still relevant in ou advanced years. Bruce asked him what key he sang Th Animals' hit *We Gotta Get Out Of This Place* in. Eri replied, 'I don't know, pick a couple and I'll find it.' A he often said he is not a technical musician.

Springsteen said that The Animals' hits had inspire his musical direction. This meant a lot to Eric, but bein the perfectionist he is, there was one thing that marre this special event for him. Back stage they ha instructed him to enter stage left and Springsteen wa expecting him from stage right, causing som momentary confusion. Now, who but an obsessiv would complain about a detail like that? Maybe th perfectionism goes back to his Tyneside roots agair where the standards of workmanship were so high, ship fitter putting a finish on a piece of mahogany in luxury liner cabin would be seen to re-sharpen his chise every time he made a cut.

'Cornflakes and curry, but not at the same time' wa once Eric's answer to the question, 'what do you eat' Nominally English, Eric makes a great cup of tea bu only when you can convince him to use one teabag i each cup instead of sharing it between two cup. Nothing is better than sitting out on the patio in th shade drinking our English tea and listening to CDs o a beat up portable CD player. Music that might includ the likes of The International Sweethearts of Rhythn Buddy Guy, Amy Winehouse and miscellaneous late forties and early-fifties bands.

Eric's musical taste today is varied, ranging all ove the musical sphere. He doesn't play much of his ow stuff other than in the car. If one of his songs comes o his tendency is to launch into a running critica commentary of his own performance.

Although he is knowledgeable about the origins of th blues in the American musical landscape, listening t obscure and primitive old stuff rarely appeals to hir much. My own collection features Alan Lomax's fiel recordings like *Murderer's Home*, 'Mississippi' Joh Hurt, Jim Jackson, 'Blind' Blake, Charlie Patton and fiel

The Animals, 1965 (ANL/Rex Shutterstock).

recordings from the 1930s along with a healthy dose of more recent stuff by Junior Kimbrough, R.L. Burnside and Cedell Davis. I love the stuff. I'm not saying Eric doesn't like it, he likes R.L, and he recognises the value, t just does not seem to be his driving passion. His mind seems to be always in the future, creating new things.

The Eric Burdon of today is also nothing like the Eric Burdon of the sixties. It's clear when you read any of Keith Altham's interviews with Eric from that period, perhaps he mellowed with age or perhaps he never was really that way. A secret of his staying power is that he eats healthily. He still has cornflakes for breakfast, but now it's with blueberries at 8am, not with whiskey at 1pm like in the sixties.

MARIANNA

Fifteen years ago, Eric met a young Greek girl called Marianna Proestou. They have been together ever since, she's now his wife and manager. They met in Germany while Eric was on a European tour. I must confess I was not enthusiastic about Marianna when we first met at Eric's 60th birthday bash at the El Ray Theater on Wilshire Blvd in Los Angeles. She was twenty-two or twenty-three then, good looking, but insecure and at the time I felt she was a little hostile. My first thought was the disparity in age and the adage; 'No fool like an old fool' however I said nothing, Eric was happy, why spoil it?

We next met when Eric played at John Asquagas Nugget Casino Hotel in Sparks, Nevada. We had all ordered breakfast; except Marianna who didn't seem to like anything on the menu. Later, that same day I drove them over to Shepler's Western Wear in Reno because Marianna wanted a pair of cowboy boots – what an ordeal! Eric and I sat for more than two hours while Marianna tried on just about every boot in the store. The problem was her feet were two different sizes! The outcome was Eric buying two pairs of boots in order to get one pair that fitted Marianna's feet. At the time I thought, 'Christ, this is the last thing he needs!'

Looking back now, I must confess I seriously misjudged Marianna. She is the best thing that has happened in Eric's tumultuous and turbulent life. Today, there could not be a person more devoted to Eric. She pulled him from the self-described 'shack' he lived in and got him into a decent house on the outskirts of Joshua Tree. She became his manager, as well as wife and she organises everything in the minutest detail – nursing Eric through his asthmatic spells and assiduously watching his health. Wife, manager, tour organiser, road manager, nurse, secretary, accountant – what could be better than that? Well, apart from the accountant bit.

Eric is very fit for his age, but the usual ailments of advancing years do require occasional attention. Bouts of rheumatism and a sensitive skin keep Marianna on the alert. At his last check-up his doctor told him to be aware of being exposed to intense sun for prolonged periods. A recent concert performance in Seattle placed him in extreme discomfort, he appeared onstage at 3pm under an unusually blistering sun and battled through his agony. He told me 'We figured it's Seattle, rain for sure, how sunny can it be? I felt like a bloody fly being burnt to a crisp under a magnifying glass.' With hoodie bandana and sunglasses he had to wrap up so much he looked like a highly animated mummy in front of an audience which was happy, but oblivious to his discomfort.

Since becoming his business manager, Marianna has taken some undeserved comments from fans complaining how she limits access to him at shows. In fact she is doing her job by changing one of Eric's long standing habits. He would generously interact with fans for up to two hours after a gruelling performance on stage. It was punishing for his health but he never complained. 'I like people and I still get a lot of that action on the road' he said 'but I really love the peace and quiet when I get home.'

Eric loves movies and one evening, while Marianna is away we want to watch a DVD. Over the wood burning fireplace, is a fifty-five inch 'smart' 3D television. The TV is a marvel of the latest technology; it can be controlled by hand signals and gestures. Unfortunately the hand signalling doodad has been left on as the default setting by recent guests. So Eric and I, now in our seventies, end up executing bizarre and totally ineffective hand movements like Navy cadets practising semaphore. Waving hands and pointing remotes in all directions, trying to get the monster to function. I point pointlessly, with one remote until Eric casually informs me it belongs to a TV stored in the garage. 'Well, why is it on the coffee table pointing to this TV then?'

© Marianna Burdon

"EVERYTHING CHANGES AND, SOMEWHERE ALONG THE LINE, I'M CHANGING WITH IT." ERIC BURDON

Between the torrent of expletives and the frenzied capering of these two old men, we had what would make a hilarious video. Eric, in frustration, calls Marianna to navigate us through the procedure over the phone. We go through the ritual step-by-step, hang up and still can't make it work. His masculine sensitivities, little diminished by age, forbid him to call Marianna again but luck is with us some of the way. After another fifteen minutes of this demented choreography, we get it to play the wrong DVD. 'I only wanted a bloody big screen TV, not some *Star Wars* sh*t.' Marianna bless her, only wanted to get him the latest technology.

Fortunately, Eric only uses the big 3D TV to play his DVDs in the evening, at ear shattering decibel level. The only commercial channel Eric really watches is the History Channel. His DVD collection includes an extensive collection of classic Film Noire and war movies. I'm OK with *Rommel* and *The Third Man* but I can live without seeing *City of Life and Death* again. I had to excuse myself several times for a fake bathroom break from the more harrowing scenes of that movie. Eric wasn't fazed, he had already seen it and thought I would like it, which is usually the case, but not this time.

Eric's expanding movie collection can be the source of marital friction. One day we drove to the Barnes & Noble in nearby Ventura to look for a particular war movie. By the time he was finished, Eric ended up with about 6 DVDs. After getting the receipt he said, 'Crap, we'd better hide this, Marianna is always at me for spending too much on movies.' 'Why? She gets the bill anyway' I said. 'I know, but it heads it off for a while.' I realised, I do exactly the same thing when I go over my limit for books on Amazon. I know my wife will get the bill eventually, but I stave off telling her when a book arrives for a few days, also heading it off for a while. It seems as if both our spouses believe you only needs a certain amount of DVDs or books in your life.

It was Eric that put me in this predicament, as it was him that got me together with my wife more than half a century ago. We were at the Majestic Ballroom on Westgate Rd in Newcastle one day in the late fifties. The Majestic was the place to be for the local teens at the time. We would take in our favourite records of the day for the resident DJ to play and we danced to them sort of li[ke] Northern England teens *Dick Clark's American Bandsta[nd]* The DJs always refused to play the records Eric an[d] brought in. 'No R&B at the Majestic son, p*ss off.'

I was on the stage talking to Eric when I noticed a s[uper] good looking girl with mauve coloured hair on the da[nce] floor. I nudged Eric and uttered the tender and fate[ful] words 'I wouldn't mind having a go at that one,' a phr[ase] probably heard more than once in the male wo[rld] particularly in Rock & Roll. He said, 'I know a frien[d of] hers, I'll fix you up if you like.' Of course I liked, and f[ifty] plus years later the mauve hair colour is long gone [but] she is still a looker – frying eggs for breakfast in [the] kitchen while Eric makes yet another cup of watery te[a].

One day last year, Eric brought one of the early cut[s of] his (at the time) unreleased new album '*Til Your Ri[ver] Runs Dry* into the living room for me to listen to. 'Th[ere] are two tracks here that I don't like' he said 'and I do[n't] think they should be included on the final album, j[ust] listen to the lot and tell me which two tracks you th[ink] they are.' While somewhat daunting, I also knew whate[ver] tracks I picked he had made his mind up already anyw[ay]. I sat in the living room with his ever-present B[ose] headphones on and listened in silence to all fourte[en] tracks, Eric on the other side of the room occasion[ally] looking over for any tell-tale signs I might reveal with [my] expressions. I'm not sure why he did this, maybe it w[as] to get an average person's input because I am no mu[sic] expert, I know what I like – but that's it. My whole car[eer] has been the design and construction of casinos.

After listening to the album it was the final two tra[cks] I didn't like, only because I thought they included so[me] now outdated references, they were more from anot[her] era and somehow lacked the energy of the other tra[cks] which had a fresh new feel. 'I didn't like the last t[wo] tracks as well as the others Eric' I said. The response w[as] swift. 'Marianna', he yelled into the kitchen, 'what di[d I] tell you, I told you those last two tracks didn't belong [on] the bloody album.' Silence from Marianna – who soldi[ers] on in Eric's life – in the kitchen, and a huge sigh of re[lief] from me. He can be a bit of a 'silly bugger' sometimes, [but] his instincts are spot on. The released album is min[us] those two songs.

(David Hepworth)

© Marianna Burdon

Clockwise from top left: 1) *'Captain' Eric Burdon.* 2) *The well-stocked vintage juke box.* 3) *Burdon in hiding.*
4) *"No R&B at the Majestic son, p*ss off!!" – now modern indie bands play at the O2 Academy, the former Majestic Ballroom.*

SECRETS OF SURVIVAL

Tuesday, 9 April, 2013. I arrive at the Ventura Amtrak station for the fifth time – I like the no hassle experience of riding Amtrak, it's so superior to flying, if you have plenty of time. There's no security, you can walk on board seconds before departure with no luggage check, or restrictions on using electrical devices, quiet and smooth as silk. Usually, Eric or Marianna is there to pick me up, but this time no one is here.

After waiting about thirty minutes I send a text to Marianna. 'Are you OK?' I ask, 'I am – Eric is not!' I had just read her reply when a Red '58 Ford pickup came screaming down the street, it was Eric, he had missed the exit off the 101 freeway somehow and got lost. 'They moved the bloody freeway sign,' he said. 'You keep an eye out for it going back, I bet the bugger is not there.' I'm wondering how I could do that when we would be heading in the opposite direction on the freeway, never mind, I'm in Eric's world now.

The classic pickup runs great but we both have to scream at each other to be heard over the engine and wind noise. Just outside Ojai, we stop to buy some fish for dinner at a popular local roadside stand. 'I need enough for three people' Eric said to the girl at the window, 'whatever *that* is.' We scream off again toward his house. Marianna's vigilance has no 'off' switch – 'there's enough for six people here Eric' she says, 'Well, I asked for three didn't I?' said Eric defiantly, looking at me for verification. 'Yes, he did say three' I chime in unconvincingly.

Over dinner, the discussion turns to Greece where Marianna likes to visit her family when there is no conflict with Eric's engagements, it's been a while since the last visit. 'What about going to Greece before we get busy touring again?' she asks. I watch Eric try to find the intransigence and stubbornness that used to make headlines, to no avail. He goes on to claim that the climate, heavy humidity and intense sun get him down, explaining that the provision of air-conditioning (apart from in five-star hotels) is sparse. As ever, it is pre-ordained who will win this one and they are both in Greece as I write.

A recent visit to the doctor for a routine check-up gave Eric a good bill of health again this time around 'Heart of a twenty year old I've got' Eric boasted to me. Checking for any signs of memory problems, the doctor asked questions like 'Do you know where you live? What is your phone number? What date is it? These were bloody silly questions according to Eric, 'of course I don't.' He hasn't got memory problems, he doesn't know his own phone number or his zip code because Marianna takes care of all this for him.

He got some shots for hand pain to help him get through an upcoming gig in El Cajon, his right hand damaged from fifty years of shaking and slapping the tambourine. Last night he told me he didn't go to sleep until 3am because of the pain, he added 'You know, I blame acid for most of my sleepless nights, have you ever had a feeling like, if you take the weight off your feet the earth will fly up to the sun and all of us with it?' – 'I'll watch out for that Eric,' I reply.

When we set out on our walk this morning, the local utility company was cutting down some of the larger trees in the front yard to prevent fire or something, because branches are tangled with the power lines. At first Eric was not fond of the large oaks found all over this area of California, 'they make me feel closed in' he said, 'I could see a big sky in Joshua Tree.' Now, conversely, he has adjusted to his new landscape and dictates to the hapless crew on what they can and cannot cut.

The summer and fall of this year is blocked for touring engagements and Eric is a little apprehensive

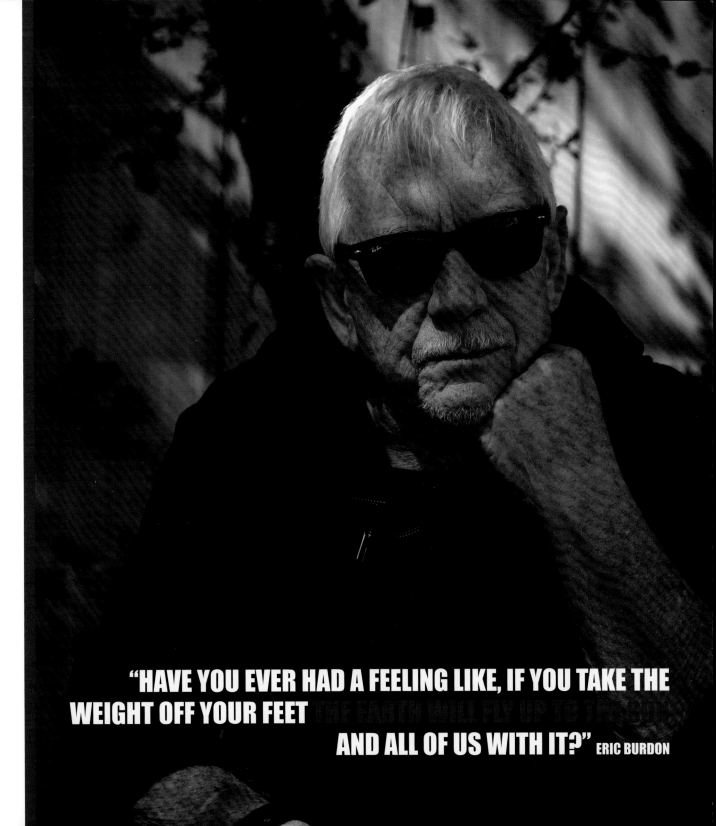

"HAVE YOU EVER HAD A FEELING LIKE, IF YOU TAKE THE WEIGHT OFF YOUR FEET THE EARTH WILL FLY UP TO THE SKY AND ALL OF US WITH IT?" ERIC BURDON

about the upcoming European gigs and interviews in the UK. 'I hope they go well,' he says, 'I don't want to be dragging around Europe like some ancient f*cking dinosaur. Plus, I prefer not to go back to England until I can kick ass.'

His newly released album, '*Til Your River Runs Dry* is showing strength and getting pretty good reviews and it turned out he was very well received in his home country. All was well.

Marianna is off to St Lucia for a few days for a women's business conference so we get the house to ourselves for a while. On the first morning we are on our own, the distinctive and intoxicating smell of the sixties drifts across the room. We discuss his new book and anecdotes for inclusion about The Beatles, The Stones and Nina Simone. The overall theme is slowly being defined – it's about Eric's life journey with more emphasis on the asthma that percolates through it.

Eric usually prepares his own breakfast; cereal, then eggs, usually fried. He likes to cook and does so as though he was servicing cannon at the Battle of Trafalgar, not quite stripped to the waist, but certainly with a sweat rag around his head. The 'Wolf' stainless steel designer pans are not his favourites and his Geordie accent starts to re-emerge when he gets frustrated. 'A've got ter put me gloves on ter fry me fockin' eggs' he says, 'the heat gans straight up the handle.' He vows to chuck them out while Marianna is gone, but we'll see. This leads to a general criticism of all the kitchenware. 'Am gettin' rid of this toy cutlery 'n all', he says, 'look at these tiny fockin' forks!' Three days later when looking in the back of the drawer for something, I saw normal sized cutlery and realised the tiny forks we had been using were dessert forks. Knowing Eric too well, I'm best to say nothing.

We make a trip to the local Vons supermarket for supplies, two 'forbidden' items feature on the list we wrote up, sea-salted potato chips and white socks. Marianna has an aversion to white socks. It is long and convoluted story involving Greeks that I have never been able to figure out. Unless it's something to do with

the quite bizarre Greek ceremonial Presidential Guard the Evzones, who wear long white socks, two on eac leg coupled with pom-poms on their shoes. 'I just hav black socks and I hate wearing them' Eric protests, 'I fee like New York mafia, walking around the 'hoose' in m shorts and black socks.' Near a candy rack, I find display with some cream-coloured 'organic' socks (afte all, this is California), and I think they will preserve th household harmony. 'They're not actually white, Eric' say. 'True' says he, 'no argument there.'

On the way back to the house we visit the local Englis 'Tea Shoppe' where Eric roams the shelves for kippers Spam, PG Tips & Tetley's tea, pickled onions and Tate Lyle treacle. The treacle can is leaking exactly like the did decades ago in England when we were kids.

Several days later Marianna is due to arrive back fron St. Lucia, so it's time to clear out all signs of sea-salte potato chips and Spam. Eric pauses, reflecting for moment. 'I've got to do this now or it'll never be done he says. He drags some artwork he received from a fa out of the storage in the garage. Not everything from th old house is unpacked yet. It's a black and re rectangular piece that we start to hang in the dinin room. The subject is a black raven in a rusty barbed wir frame. I measure it and centre it over the fireplace an start to hang it. Typically of Eric he says 'That's not *m* centre, *my* centre is here', pointing to the centre joint i the place I had already determined. 'You can't have *tw* centres Eric, centre is centre' I say. 'Well, *I* can', h responds. Perhaps another key to his survival is any an all things are open to any and all interpretation. Eric universe is always rapidly expanding in randon directions.

It's 7.30am, May 13, 2013. I'm back at home in La Vegas and Eric is on the phone from his hotel room i New York. 'I'm back and I'm p*ssed,' he says. 'Wha happened man?' I ask. 'Just joking, I thought it woul be a good title for an album, the cover could be me wit my back to the camera. We got back last night, killed i in London and Spain and *the other place*.' The othe place being Greece of course. He's still a sh*t-stirrer, bu

Eric Burdon and Chas Chandler, 1964. (Clifford Ling/Rex Shutterstock)

he was happy and things had obviously gone well. 'Loads of interviews in London and New York,' he said. The interviews in London apparently went well, but he expressed disappointment at not being able to hook up with Keith Altham, the well-known PR 'go to guy' for the rock stars of the sixties and seventies. Keith wrote articles for the English *New Musical Express* and other trade journals at the time and although he could have a biting tongue he was always kindly disposed towards Eric. 'I'm bummed I couldn't get hold of Keith,' Eric said.

While in New York he was happy with his meetings with record company executives, 'they treated me real good,' he said – surprised. He still nurses corporate bruises from the recording industry, but he was sounding good. Another of his survival secrets is he never ever expects the best, but always questions both the best and the worst. 'Got to get back to the book though' (his autobiography) he said. 'I might drive over to your place when we get back to California.' For someone who regularly gets lost in his own neighbourhood, this conjured up a bit of an alarming picture for me.

The immediate task at hand is typing everything he has written longhand, which he is able to do not only at speed but with brilliant simplicity that requires little editing. We slog away at the book again with me trying to collate Eric's torrent of words and recollections. Starting on 'The Toon' (Geordie for 'The town' or Newcastle) where we grew up and the crucible which left Eric with the same capacity for change in character as Jurassic limestone.

'That's not my centre!' Fan artwork mounted by Burdon and Payne.

"I'M BACK AND I'M P*SSED – JUST JOKING, I THOUGHT IT WOULD BE A GOOD TITLE FOR AN ALBUM"

"I'VE BEEN LIVING PURE FICTION SO I MIGHT AS WELL TRY WRITING SOME." ERIC BURDON

© Marianna Burdon

THE 'TOON'

Eric and I come from the cold, north east corner of England. Very different from the rest of England, it is heavy with Scots and Scandinavian history and influence, particularly in the local dialect, like the name of the inhabitants, also known as 'Geordie'. Geordie has many words derived from the Angles who sailed over from Jutland in the sixth century. The Britons they were driving out and replacing spoke a sort of Welsh sounding Gaelic. These early invaders came in boats and settled in the North East area, violently displacing the indigenous locals.

I was born on 7 May 1940 and Eric on 11 May 1941. We are both Geordies of course, the common description for the inhabitants of the large, industrial city of Newcastle upon Tyne. Our birthplace has a long and violent history. Originally a Roman settlement, the Norman invaders of 1066 built a castle there in 1080, a 'new' castle from which the city derives its name. The North East was repeatedly invaded by the Anglo Saxons of Europe, the Vikings of Norway, the Danes and the murderous Picts from Scotland, all of whom settled there after driving out the original inhabitants.

There are more fortifications, castles and military ruins there than anywhere else in England. Eric and I feel we share in this blood-drenched ancestry. The Geordie dialect today still retains traces of the foreign invaders' languages. When we are alone, we sometimes revert to the Geordie dialect just for fun, and to test each other's fading memories. I suggested to Eric that a small portion of his forthcoming book could be written in Geordie and he looked at me as if I was the one on acid this time. Instead he *'hoyed 'iz in the ootside nettie and ah got hacky and clarty then he hockled off the cracket where he was porched on his hunkers, I was varnigh dozzend.'* This roughly translates as 'He threw me into the outside lavatory and I became encrusted with dirt and detritus, he then spat upon the small wooden stool, where he was sat upon his haunches, I was very nearly shrunken.' I saw his point, Geordie won't work.

The foregoing strangled statement might be understood by the following luminaries, all of whom hail from Newcastle and its immediate environs - Stan Laurel (lived in North Shields for a spell), Mr Bean Rowan Atkinson, Sting, Cheryl Cole, Bryan Ferry, Brian Johnson of AC/DC, Mark Knopfler, Hank Marvin, Sir Joseph Swan – inventor of the incandescent light bulb (sorry America), architectural structural engineer Ove Arup, Jimmy Nail, Ridley Scott, actor Bill Travers, Sid Chaplin, Catherine Cookson and engineering giant George Stephenson.

Perhaps Eric was predestined to be in the music business as he had songwriters and entertainers in his family history. The author of the famous song (at least to Geordies everywhere) *Blaydon Races*, the de facto Geordie anthem, was Eric's great-great uncle George (or Geordie) Ridley, who had been a miner in the mid-1800s. His distant relative did not receive any royalties from the song. As well as both losing out on royalties for songs synonymous with their names, there are a lot of similarities between these two relatives.

Both were born on Tyneside of course, George Ridley in 1835 and Eric in 1941. Ridley's father was called Matthew as was Eric's dad. *Blaydon Races* was published almost exactly one hundred years before *The House of the Rising Sun* hit the charts. George Ridley, started as a child coalmine worker in the mid-1800s. Working in this environment may have caused the respiratory problems which were supposedly 'miraculously' cured in one week by a visiting American medical promoter called Dr Airy. Eric has been plagued with asthma since childhood, but he has not found a miracle cure.

Both George and Eric share powerful singing voices and George sourced American black and minstrel tunes for his songs, music which he obviously liked, while Eric's interest and interpretations of American blues and R&B permeates his musical repertoire. George wrote a song about a character he knew – Joe Hogg. Eric, as a teen, had a close friend called Jackie 'Animal' Hogg who inspired The Animals' name. George was also interested in the visual arts, as a boy, after his shift at the pit, he

Newcastle, early 1960s. The Tyne Bridge with Armstrong's innovative Swing Bridge in the foreground. Eric's paternal grandfather was a 'pilot' on the rotating bridge.

would amuse friends and family by cutting out paper figures, putting a cloth across the front of his rabbit hutch and performing a puppet show of his own creation. Eric got his degree in graphic design and is a respected visual artist.

George had songs performed by the Royal Fusiliers Pipe Band, Eric had a Scots Dragoons band playing in the background of his hit *Sky Pilot*. George was 'cheated' out of major financial gain from his songs by Robert Allen, a Newcastle stationer who made lots of money from subsequent publishing of George's song writing. Eric feels 'cheated' out of *The House of the Rising Sun* royalties.

Talk about history repeating itself. George Ridley died age twenty-nine; thank God Eric is still going. Sting, another Geordie lad, recorded *Cushy Butterfield* another number written by Eric's great-great uncle.

Shipbuilding cranes dominate the skyline, Wallsend, 1949.

Clockwise from above: 1) *Mounted on the side of the William IV public house, Gateshead, a blue plaque commemorates Burdon's great-great uncle.* 2) *Testing mechanical pit props at Westoe Colliery, South Shields, 1965.* 3) *Geordies at the Hydraulic Crane pub, Scotswood, 1962.* 4) *Beneath huge steel girders, Geordies crouch in the foundations of the King Edward VII Bridge, 1905.*

BORN IN AN AIR RAID

Like most expatriate Geordies we have a love-hate relationship with Newcastle upon Tyne. It was industrially grimy (although now greatly improved) and the weather pretty much uniformly miserable. It has been economically depressed for 100 years and seems sometimes to be permanently so. It's a tough place, but it's still 'wor' roots; the place that formed us, for better or worse.

Eric was born during a German air raid on Newcastle, I was born in 1940, only four months before the front of our house was blown off by a bomb. Growing up, the war shaped our lives, both of us having to hide in air raid shelters and wear gas masks for the first years of our lives. Neither of us will forget the frightening and mournful sound of the air raid warning siren. Eric remembers the gas masks for babies operated by hand bellows; talking about it later, we discovered we both used them as 'space helmets'.

Even though Newcastle had shipbuilding and armaments factories, we were never evacuated to the so-called safety of the Orwellian sounding 'reception areas'. Some urban areas did evacuate children, but it did not work perfectly because families kept bringing their kids back home if the bombing eased up, only to send them back when it intensified again. Some families welcomed the evacuated kids, others did not. Some even abused them, but fortunately others treated them better than the home they were evacuated from. Some responded to receiving the evacuees with a sense of humour. I read an account of a man who purportedly wrote to the Ministry of Health saying 'Returning: one small boy, please send bomb instead!' Our parents were told by the government that the evacuations were necessary to 'ensure preservation of the next generation'.

Kids like Eric and I, not being evacuated, endured terrible anxiety and fear. The noise and danger of the air raids, sleepless nights in the musty, dark air raid shelters, together with the possibility of being bombed out and witnessing death, destruction and maiming all around us. At first it was an adventure, the adrenalin rush of the warning siren, tumbling into the shelter, cheering when we saw a bomber get 'coned' by searchlights. The thrill of the 'all clear' and getting out on the street to collect still-warm shrapnel. Then, after a bomb came close, it became real fear.

In our ignorance, as kids, adventure was mixed with fear, however the adults never knew when it was their turn to be blasted to smithereens, or whether the neighbours would still exist after the all clear. Because fathers and male relations were at war and mothers were working in the factories, there was little adult supervision during this time. We just ran wild on the bomb sites. It wasn't all fun, occasionally kids would drown playing in the static water tanks placed on the streets to supply water for putting out fires from incendiary bombs. Eric told me about a friend of his who suffocated playing hide and seek in the large sand boxes placed around town for the same purpose. But it was always exciting to play in the blasted ruins of someone's kitchen or living room.

It was a big adjustment for us kids when, after the war, a large hairy guy in thick and scratchy clothes came back into our lives. My father was a strict disciplinarian, he (like Eric's Uncle Jack), was a Regimental Sergeant Major in the army. My father treated us with withering discipline, ordering us around like subordinates in the forces. These newly 'demobbed' fathers brought back strangled English phrases from distant arenas of war. I remember we called our bread knife a 'gully' and Eric will still on occasion to this day come out with a 'can I do you now sir?' from the radio show It's That Man Again.

Because of years with little parental control, the period immediately following the war saw a huge rise in juvenile crime in England by kids just a few years older than Eric and I. After the war the whole country endured a period of acute deprivation until rationing ended in the early fifties. Eric and I were young teens when the end of sweet (candy) rationing came about in 1954. The result of this was we could only have what was available in food, clothing and entertainment, and there wasn't much of any of that. If you are formed by the first few years of your life, then these are the conditions that formed Eric and me.

Incredible as it seems to me now, when I started school at four years old in 1944 we sat on the floor, everyone had a slate writing board & chalk and the teacher put coal on the classroom fire. Eric attended Wharrier Street School in Walker. He thought the name meant something to do with warriors (it might be named after a person called Wharrier) and to avoid any imagined confrontations he would hide in the school toilets until the classes started. It was located between a slaughterhouse and the shipyards, which soon were to become the target of German bombing.

As children, we probably did not quite understand what was going on during the war and its aftermath, but there were so many fun places to play – bombed and blasted rubble piles, demolished houses to play cowboys and indians in, shattered trees to climb, underground air raid shelters in the garden to use as forts and gas masks turned into monsters or spacemen masks. For the adults, wood salvaged from the bombed houses could be used for heating if necessary instead of scarce coal. Toilet paper was almost non-existent, we had the *Daily Mirror* on a string in our 'netty' (toilet). Even though food rationing stayed in effect until 1953, we never felt deprived of anything – as children of the welfare state we were actually pretty healthy. Our parents were being inventive with leftovers, bread & dripping, mashed potato and Spam of course. A can of which Eric has in his kitchen, as do I – cue song '*Old habits die hard.*'

As teens, smoking was the cool thing. The upstairs of the 'double-decker' buses so thick with cigarette smoke it was hard to see. It seemed everyone smoked, even in the cinema, all peering at the screen through a blue haze. I tried to smoke a pipe and still remember the occasion in the dark of the cinema when I turned the pipe over and the burning tobacco fell into my lap. I went back to 'tabs' (cigarettes) after that. Because of his concerns about his asthma, Eric never smoked.

Although we were both born in Newcastle, Eric's family could be described as a little better off than mine because his dad, Matt, had a regular job with the National Electricity Board. Eric tells me that his dad was a good father to him, supportive, instructive and vehemently anti-war. What we might call a conscientious objector, an anti-war attitude which made an impression on the young Eric. My family leaned toward the bottom of the social economic scale, being descendants of refugees who fled to England during the Irish potato famine of the mid-1800s. On my mother's side there was a dysfunctional family of alcoholics; my father deserted the family for female pastures new when I was around six years old.

Marondale Avenue in Walker, where Eric lived, consisted of up and down council flats (apartments) on quite a pleasant street that had actual gardens. I lived in a colliery row house in Riddle Terrace in Coxlodge, a mining suburb of Newcastle, no gardens front or back and dozens of mines in the area. The whole of the Tyneside area including Walker, had mining operations and collieries and was riddled with coal seams. Due to the particular nature of the coal mined on Tyneside, hundreds of lives were lost over the decades due to coal dust and 'firedamp' explosions. Even through the fifties, newspaper stories would occasionally appear about a street or a house collapsing into an old coal seam.

Newcastle and its inhabitants were, and still are to a large extent, ignored by the government when it comes to handing out public largess. As Geordies it seems we were of little consequence. Winston Churchill said years earlier of the striking Geordie miners who led the Jarrow hunger marches, 'let them eat grass' comparing the inhabitants of our area to cattle. As young teens we were oblivious to this harsh history, although we heard the older folks talk about the hard times. We all knew of the hunger marches, but we were more interested in knowing when the Quadrini's ice cream van would be navigating the washing strung out between houses in the grimy back lanes where we played.

Eric told me that in Walker, a man with a horse and cart came around accompanied by a monkey, and for a penny you could go for a ride on the cart. Horses and carts were still a common sight in the early fifties in Newcastle. The coalman, the milkman, rag & bone man and the knife sharpener all plied their trade with a horse and cart. The knife sharpener sometimes came around on a modified bicycle and he would sharpen any knife or blade you gave him. Every two weeks, the 'French onion' man came around with bundles of onions hanging over the handlebars of his bicycle. I never worked out whether it was him or the onions that were

Top: *Destruction in Newcastle following an air raid.* Above left: *Fitting gas masks, 1941.* Above right: *Eric's street, Marondale Avenue in Walker, seen in 2015.*

French, or both. Of course, Eric swears contrarily, that the French onion man was Spanish.

As kids we were seldom in the house; we played in the back streets until it was too dark to see, and on wastelands of cleared bombsites and slag heaps – the mountains of rubbish and detritus from the coal mines. We still had chimney sweeps in those days and as kids we would be sent outside to shout out when the sweeps brush popped out of the top of the chimney.

Eric and I both collected American horror comics; we preferred them to the English comic fare of *The Dandy*, *Beano*, *Korky the Cat* and *Desperate Dan*. Horror was where the action was for us, nothing like getting a new *Tales from the Crypt*. Eric sometimes traded his comics for military artefacts like German head gear and hand grenades, and Eric being Eric, hoped for live ones. I traded mine in for books I didn't get as a child. I was gutted when my mother took my entire collection of horror comics from under my bed and threw them out. The British Government had decided that American horror comics were degenerate and poisoning the youth of England. Eric's comics suffered the same fate but Eric, as usual suspecting a conspiracy, suggested that the government probably had some vested interest in the *Dandy* or *Beano*.

We left school at fifteen. This was the mid-fifties which was a great time for us, just as Rock & Roll was bursting onto the music scene. We didn't know that at the time of our birth, the seeds were being sown for Chuck Berry, Elvis Presley and Little Richard by artists like blues harmonica player Bill Gillum, boogie-woogie pianist Albert Ammons and pianist and rockabilly singer Moon Mullican who were performing embryonic Rock & Roll in the late-thirties and early-forties. We didn't know it then, but the Shelton Brothers' recording of *Aura Lee* is Elvis Presley's *Love Me Tender* and Arthur Crudup had written and recorded *That's all right* long before Elvis did.

Harker's Army Surplus store was on the corner of Percy Street in Newcastle. It was a favourite browsing place of Eric as a youngster and sold everything in the way of military hardware and equipment, Eric would keep us informed by with a running commentary on the store's inventory. Also on Percy Street, was a sheepskin curing warehouse where wagons piled high with sheep carcasses would arrive every day. The entrance was open to the street and the stench from the place was terrible. I can only imagine what it would smell like on a hot day, fortunately they were pretty rare.

When Eric and I were teenagers, a great place for liv music was the Newcastle City Hall where a lot of b names performed. In 1957 alone, when Eric was sixtee almost seventy shows or acts appeared at Newcastle Ci Hall including Count Basie, Buddy Holly and the Cricket Muddy Waters, Kid Ory, Sister Rosetta Tharpe and El Fitzgerald. They even put something on in 1959 billed the Newport Jazz Festival, which featured Dizzy Gillesp and Dave Brubeck among others. So there was plenty stuff around that framed our interest in music. Early the fifties, Newcastle City Hall turned down Nat Kir Cole for the strange reason that 'Jazz fans are to rowdy.'

There was also a place on Pilgrim Street in Newcast where we all went to hang out whenever we could. It ha been called the Socialist Hall but the name had bee changed to the Mahogany Hall after a venue in Ne Orleans. A couple of big names playing there aroun 1955 were 'Big' Bill Broonzy and Josh White. Like 'Big' B Broonzy, Eric has always had a theatrical bent in h choice of personal attire, a sort of restrained Keit Richards look. Eric dislikes stage suits describing the as too confining and not his kind of thing at all. Aft more than 50 years, although now continuously implore by Marianna, Eric refuses to dress up for stag performances invoking his memory of 'Big' Bill Broon always performing in his regular street clothes. What wa good enough for 'Big' Bill is good enough for him.

By the late fifties, Eric formed his first band, Th Pagans, with his friend from Newcastle College of A John Steel, on drums. The band entered a contest perform at the Empire Theatre in Newcastle on *Th Carroll Levis Discovery Show*. They didn't win, but it wa a start. I still have a photo of us all celebrating back John's house on Egremont Drive in Gateshead, a popul gathering place for us, above the Fish & Chip shop, an between The Three Tuns and The Traveller's Rest pub After *The Carroll Levis Discovery Show*, we got legle drunk, a bottle of Newcastle Brown Ale can be seen the bedroom dresser in the background of th photograph, a bottle that never reached our lips as I trie to pick it up with boxing gloves on. John Steel remembe his biggest problem at this show was fighting to stop h drum kit from a slow slide into the orchestra pit. W didn't know a theatre stage slopes from the back dow to the footlights.

Top: At John Steel's house in Gateshead following the performance at The Carroll Levis Discovery Show. *(Left to right: 'Whitey', Philip Payne, John Steel and Dave Ashcroft).* Bottom left: *Author Philip J. Payne and Eric Burdon pose with the Mayor of Newcastle's Limousine, today the Mayor has an environmentally friendly Nissan Leaf with the same registration number.* Bottom right: *Philip Payne and Winston Scott at College.*

Geordies with attitude, Payne and Burdon at college.

CLAYTON ROAD COLLEGE OF ART

lthough we only lived a few short miles apart, Eric and first met while we were at Newcastle College of Art & ndustrial Design on Clayton Road in Newcastle. A huge ld Victorian pile, which at the time still housed a lot of he original fantastically ornate Victorian furniture left ver from previous occupants. Immediately next door the college by some stroke of divine providence, tood the mansion of the Lord Mayor of Newcastle. Two f the most incompatible neighbours. Eric and I would ess about with his majestic old black Mayoral Rolls oyce, usually parked outside by the kerb, using it for npromptu photo shoots and other 'artistic' activities, ke painting eyeballs on the headlights.

John Steel, The Animals' future drummer and fellow tudent, was very much a jazz fan and although Eric had ifferent musical interests, they hit it off right away. ohn was, and still is, a naturally friendly fellow who got n with most folks.

It can be said that the art colleges in England in the fties and sixties were largely repositories for those ho felt formal apprenticeships in the local trades were eneath their dignity. They perhaps thought of them as form of slavery, factory jobs to them were anathema. rt college seemed to be for all those square pegs who idn't fit into round holes. It's not really surprising that lot of British rock music artists had an art college ducation. Sharing a common interest in music and love f obscure movies caused John, Eric and I to become ast friends.

It's amazing any of us graduated from the art college onsidering the endless hours we spent at the movies hen we should have been in class. During the day it as cartoon fare at the Tatler Cinema on Iorthumberland Street, a place in which Eric, Winston another friend) and I must have spent months while we hould have been attending college. In the evening our avourite cinema was The Stoll on Westgate Road. It was eedier than the other cinemas in town but offered uch more interesting stuff to us. It had a reputation

for showing movies that were out of the mainstream and the only place in Newcastle to show what the British at the time called 'X' movies. The 'X' designation was more for violence than sex.

In the sixties, while the Odeon Cinema might be playing *The Sound of Music*, or 'Sound of Mucus' as we called it, the Stoll would be showing *Naked as Nature Intended*, starring Anita Ekberg, or *The Wild Leather Boys*. We loved it, it was to The Stoll Eric dragged me to see *Kanal* and *Ashes and Diamonds*, both dark and unflinchingly brutal movies for the time. He is still doing this to me today only with DVDs – now I think about it, like the movie *City of Life and Death*.

We also saw Brigitte Bardot for the first time at The Stoll in *And God Created Woman*; this raised our carnal expectations of the lasses of Newcastle to an unrealistically high level. Brigitte Bardot may have been a little remote for us, but England did have its own glamour icons. The busty Diana Dors for example, and the super unnaturally busty, Sabrina.

Diana Dors was an actual movie actress, you could not say the same for Sabrina – with a figure so outlandish her career was limited to magazine spreads, walk on appearances on TV comedy shows and commercials. We didn't care, she had massive breasts!

The Queen's Cinema in Newcastle was the only venue back then to have the latest in movie technology for the time, Cinerama. Eric and I saw *The Robe* there, memorable because the guy in the row opposite us had a seizure of some kind and they stopped the film.

Ask him today what his favourite films are and Eric will likely come up with the same two movies. One is the 1963 movie, *Billy Liar* with Tom Courtney and Julie Christie and the other is the 1976 movie *Taxi Driver* with Robert De Nero.

At art college, Eric was an incorrigible prankster. This talent resulted in him being unjustly suspended for a Rag Week prank which was actually executed by Winston and me. We hung a full size dummy dressed in some of my Uncle Frank's old work clothes from the floodlights at St James's Park football ground, the home of Newcastle United. A picture of this appeared in the *Evening Chronicle* as someone had reported a hanging at St James's. Because of his reputation, Eric was immediately targeted by the college faculty as the miscreant who had perpetrated the prank. Of course being close and stalwart friends, Winston and I said nothing in his defence.

Although we knew we lived in an ancient town, it's only looking back now I realise we were quite oblivious to some of the ancient names and places around us. I suppose the exuberance of youth has no time for the past. There were street names in Newcastle which just rolled of our tongues as normal and unexceptional. Winston lived on Two Ball Lonnen, and Jeavons (the record and music store) which was a popular hangout place for us, was on a street called Pudding Chare. There was also Amen Corner, Dog Leap Stairs and Darn Crook. Pink Lane for some reason was a hot spot for 'ladies of the evening.'

Newcastle has been a fortified town since Roman times and had a number of entry gates, the names of which still apply to today's city streets, like Westgate Road, Newgate Street (the site of Newgate prison) and Gallowgate the site of the town gallows for public hangings. In years past, there was also a wooden gallows on the Town Moor. This needed to be frequently rebuilt as people kept chipping off bits off the wood – chewing wood chips from a gallows was thought to be an ancient cure for toothache.

By the mid-sixties, in a relentless pursuit of public modernisation, the local authorities had destroyed many of the Newcastle's fine Georgian and Regency buildings and streets in the name of progress, replacing them with 'modern', ugly concrete bunker style buildings.

Our slacking off during the day at college was followed by hard partying at night with copious amounts of Newcastle Brown Ale; girls not respected the next morning and the most painful hangovers. Sorting out whose pants belonged to who, out of about eight people in the bedroom in the deafening haze of early morning is not soon forgotten. I found it possible to sleep on the staircase, upside down, stark naked.

Below left: *Now the Tyne Theatre, The Stoll on Westgate Road showed more stimulating films than 'The Sound of Music'.* **Below right:** *Charlie and Philip at the Downbeat Club. Charlie was responsible for Eric getting his first proper 'bedroom sex', by allowing Eric and his girlfriend to use his Mam and Dad's bed while they were on holiday.*

GREAT BALLS OF FIRE

was during one of these boozy nights when Eric approached me in a decidedly weaving gait and muttered 'can you check something out?' He thought he might have caught VD (venereal disease) as we called sexually transmitted diseases then. For some reason, I was considered the expert among us on matters sexual (not that I got a lot, but I was getting more than the others it seems).

I had experimented with a contraceptive pessary called Ginamin, a pill about the size of a Tums. The instructions were to insert it into your 'love interest' ten minutes before intercourse. This presented the difficult task of simultaneously engaging in small talk, trying to maintain an erection and keeping your girlfriend in a state of excitement in the hope that she wouldn't change her mind for the ten interminable minutes the pessary required to reach the correct foaming consistency. You were then faced with the prospect of keeping an erection while trying to insert it into a combination of unknown chemicals designed to kill living sperm.

Eric never had any problem getting girls, they were always attracted to him, and he had something we didn't. I didn't know what it was at the time, but he had 'presence' like most famous people.

We both staggered down the stairs and out the back door to the old outside toilet in the back yard. A toilet barely the size of a telephone booth.

We stood facing each other, drunkenly swaying and Eric dropped his pants. I fished a box of Swan Vestas (The Smoker's Match) out of my pocket and struck one (the light bulb in the toilet was broken as usual). 'What do you think this is?' said Eric. I leaned forward and down and held the match close to his privates, but in doing so my back bumped into the wall behind me and I lurched forward. All I remember is a bluish flash and an acrid smell of burning hair and Eric screeching and slapping at his privates with both hands. I'm sure no

one, in the history of the world has sobered up faster than Eric did then. After all that, it turned out it was just a large boil near his testicles.

Tip: don't let drunken friends anywhere near your private parts with a live flame.

During the college years, between booze-ups we would lie around the bedroom, mostly in John Steel's parents' house. The walls were adorned with metal street signs we had ripped off walls and sign posts. We'd talk about life, music and girls. Eric would often wax lyrical, frequently about the then girl of his dreams, Rosie Booth. Rosie was a fellow student at the Art College and had a special attraction for us, especially Eric. She was barely five feet tall but perfectly formed; she styled herself after Brigitte Bardot in the movie *Doctor at Sea*.

Rosie said she first saw Eric at the college entrance. 'He was on the stairs and gave me a big grin. I thought – who is that long-haired spotty gnome and gave him *such* a look, like *as if*.' For all Rosie's reaction to him Eric never had any problem 'pulling the birds' – he had something that made people take notice and it's still there in the way he relates to the audiences today in his concert performances.

On one occasion I got fed up with hearing Eric going on about a girl who he described as 'like an unreachable diamond, a desirable jewel but behind glass' he could see but not touch. I said I thought she was a bit of a slapper and Eric, with a 'F*ck you Payne', jumped up, tore one of the metal street signs off the wall and hurled the thing in my direction. It came whirling across the room like a helicopter blade and embedded itself in the wall about three inches above my head.

I had a strong interest in early American Blues and R&B and spent a lot of time collecting obscure (at least in England at the time) American R&B and rock records. During this time Eric and John had teamed up with another couple of students and had improvised jam sessions wherever and whenever they could. I had no natural musical talent. In my early teens I had tried playing the trombone, but I just wasn't any good. Eric also started first with the trombone but with a disapproving glance from God or something, he thankfully soon abandoned it in favour of singing.

Eric and I always have shared a slightly skewed way of looking at life, probably due to our 'evil' schools a he describes them, this resulted him having a stella career in later life, while I was destined to be jus slightly skewed. Growing up in the grim surrounding of Newcastle with little prospect of grasping the 'bras ring' probably causes one to have a more skewed an cynical approach to life.

Pagans: Eric Burdon, John Steel and Dave Ashcroft. Philip Payne looking on in the background.

RADIO DAYS

For us, the radio was the only real source of entertainment with lots of soap operas, plays and half-hour comedy shows. TV was available for the relatively well-off but in the fifties there were only two black and white channels and the content always seemed to consist of a kind of faded Lawrence Welk type show and not much else. Also in the fifties, TV shut down for two hours every day between the children's programs finishing at 6pm and the adult programs starting at 8pm. There was nothing at all for teens.

There were many radio programs at the time that held our attention by being comically absurd, fostering our skewed way of looking at things. One favourite radio program while we attended college was called *The Goon Show*, an irreverent and nonsensical show put out by the usually staid and prudish BBC. It was like a radio version of *Monty Python* and featured Peter Sellers and Spike Milligan. It's surprising to me now that while the BBC pushed the boundaries of comedic surrealism they were hell-bent on not giving any exposure to Rock & Roll music.

One series on the radio was called *The Archers* which Eric, with his natural penchant toward all kinds of warfare, thought would be like Robin Hood. Eric told me he was bitterly disappointed when it turned out to be a pedestrian show, 'an everyday story of country folk' on a farm!

The American singer Frankie Laine was popular in those days, often described as 'a big lad with leather lungs and steel tonsils.' Eric loved that 'big' sound of Frankie Laine. Recently, I woke up to Eric's unmistakable voice booming Frankie Laine from the master bedroom, Rollin, Rollin, Rollin, keep them dogies rollin' – he was awake and feeling good.

In the months before we left secondary school at the age of fifteen 'job counsellors' visited to explain what jobs we could expect to do when we left school. Being what was called 'working class' the jobs outlined to us were in coal mining, shipbuilding, factories or building construction. No doctors or lawyers among this bunch of proles, they must have thought. It didn't matter anyway, our minds were already focussed on a different future of girls, girls, girls and music, music, music.

I had a friend called Malcolm 'Polly' Gibb (who got the nickname because he had the habit of repeating everything one said). He had two attractions. One, his uncle was in the merchant navy, he frequently sailed between the UK and America, and every time he came back to Newcastle he brought a slew of American records with him, mostly R&B and Rock & Roll. Two, Polly, had a good looking sister who had a reported reputation of going 'all the way'. Unfortunately, not with me as it turned out, despite my best efforts. I had already done 'it' with a girl anyway, when I was quite young in the bushes at the bottom of the soccer field at school. Well, it was penetration; it would be a serious stretch to call it sexual intercourse. 'Why has it gone floppy?' lived with me for a long time.

I would take my and Polly's records with my Dansette portable record player to art college to play during the break time in the evening in the common room where we had a couple of hours to fill in before evening class. Eric immediately connected with a Joe Turner record I brought in called *Boss of the Blues*. He loved Joe Turner and Joe Williams stuff and as it turned out he had an amazing vocal ability to sound just like them.

Where his voice came from I don't know, but even back then in those early days it was powerful and bluesy.

BECOMING ANIMALS

By the time we graduated from college Eric and the band were calling themselves The Pagans and playing in dilapidated, dismal church halls and workingmen's clubs to audiences more familiar with artists like Tommy Steel and the British pop songs of the day. This was not Animals' material. Eric's insistence on sticking to American R&B and Blues and not acquiescing to requests from the dance hall punters to play the pop hits of the day led to many an impromptu fight with members of the audience.

At one of these venues, a guy playing with another struggling band asked to sit in with the group and immediately stormed into some amazing boogie-woogie piano. It was Alan Price. Alan was a little different, always moody and a bit prickly, but what a piano player he was.

Alan Price lived in the town of Morpeth, a few miles away from Newcastle. If the rehearsals at Johnny's house went on too late and he missed the last bus home, he would sleep over at my house. At the time, my mother had an old upright piano in the living room that he would tinker about on. One morning, after he left I found a piece of scrap paper on the piano in his handwriting saying simply 'Alan Price will be a famous pianist someday.' He obviously knew where he was going. I kept the note for years after The Animals became famous, but lost it after moving to the US.

For a while, The Pagans became the Kansas City Five and frequently played the Club A Go-Go in Newcastle. Later, when Mike Jeffery (the Club A Go-Go owner) opened the Downbeat Club in Carliol Square, Eric, myself and Winston Scott, all being students at Clayton Road Art College, helped in creating the interior design of the club. Eric designed the concept and Winston and I did artwork.

During college holiday periods we launched frequent 'recreational' forays into the Northumbrian countryside to sleep rough and create general havoc. The late fifties had a liberating feeling for us, we felt it was the first time we had the ability to create our own destiny even if we didn't have a clue where to start or what our destiny was.

During the war and into the fifties, there had been minimal parental control and a lot of deprivation, and discipline was harsh at some schools in England. The teachers seemed to control their pupils exclusively by corporal punishment. Some would steal the leather straps that were used to pull up the windows in railway carriages and these became weapons in the teachers' arsenal. The straps were about four inches wide and a quarter of an inch thick. One end of the strap would be cut into short tails and used to lash you from the inside of the wrist up to the inside forearm.

Between the age of eleven and fifteen, it seemed even the most diligent student would have learned very little at my or Eric's schools. The 'evil' school he called it. Our teachers were not the cream of the crop – they were exhausted and frustrated, just trying to get through the day. In those hormonal teen years my school was segregated, with girls housed in a separate school building.

When we started college everything seemed to change at once – we started mixing with girls, Rock & Roll 'happened' and just being exposed to other cultural influences outside our narrow upbringing made for pretty heady stuff.

Each year King's College, University of Newcastle upon Tyne, held what was called Rag Week, a time when students were freed from attending classes to raise money for charity. Clayton Road Art College also participated; it was an excuse to annoy the general public with impromptu parades and events. 1959 had been designated 'World Refugee' year in order to promote public awareness of the plight of refugees. The King's College students decided to set up a sort of mini refugee camp right in the middle of town, stating that

(Jimmy Perry)

Eric Burdon singing at the Club A Go-Go, Mike Carr on Piano, Johnie Butts on Drums.

USED TO HANG OUT A LOT IN JAZZ CLUBS, AND THE GROUPS TOOK TO A
D LIKE ME WHO WASN'T AFRAID TO GET UP AND SING WITH A JAZZ BAND.
EN I STARTED TO HANG OUT IN ROCK CLUBS AND LEARNED TO CARRY
FF DIFFERENT STYLES." ERIC BURDON

they would live in these shanties for the whole week, they then challenged all the other students in town to do the same.

Eric and I got right on it, after all we had been sleeping rough out in the countryside and this was right in town, we didn't even need to travel to do this. Charity collection boxes were issued to all participants and we dived in. It was a bit of a problem for Alan Price because being a civil servant and working in the tax office, he had to be presentable during the day.

However, every day of the camp-out, as soon as the pubs opened we took a long 'beverage' break. Consequently, we spent more on beer than we would ever hope to collect in donations. It also meant we ran out of our own meagre money pretty fast and the charity collection boxes began to be viewed with covetous eyes. Eric maintains I was the first to pry open a collection box for beer money, I'm not so sure. Our rationale was the spurious argument that probably only half the money would get to the refugees anyway, so we decided to take the half we figured would never get to them. We kept up this rough sleeping for just under a week, during which Eric and I got into more than our share of fights with the locals in the nearby pubs. Eric never backed away from a fight and even instigated a few. The whole thing got to be too much eventually

(Jimmy Perry)

Eric Burdon singing with the Alan Price Combo at the Club A Go-Go, Price on the piano on the far left.

Cold, hungry and more than a little out of joint, at the end of it all, we had managed to secure for Winston – a broken wrist, Eric – a serious bowel disorder and I was in hospital with alcohol poisoning and pleurisy.

Eventually, we did manage to graduate from Clayton Road College with our National Design Degree diplomas. This feat had apparently also been achieved a few short years before us by the movie director, Ridley Scott, a local lad from the nearby town of South Shields, who attended art college in Hartlepool. On leaving college we all drifted into various day jobs. John Steel kept steady drumming gigs in addition to being in the band. Eric was singing and also laboured with his dad at the Electricity Board. I got a job with Reed Millican, a local glass manufacturer.

Despite his successful graduation, when Eric left college, one of the resident faculty, Kenneth Shuttleworth, frustrated by years of trying to get Eric to toe the line, told Eric that 'you won't amount to a bloody thing lad, you're just a waster.'

Eric could have had a successful career as a graphic artist, being good at graphic design, he's not bad as an artist/illustrator either. We both got our diploma by a squeaker by frantically cramming in the last six months of the five years we attended art school. The disparaging lecturer, Ken Shuttleworth, was still at the college a few years later when Eric rolled up in his big American convertible. On another visit to the old college, Eric told me he saw a little plaque in the common room which bore the legend 'Eric Burdon slept here.'

Every year the 'Hoppings' came to town during the summer holidays. This huge fairground sets up for two weeks on Newcastle's Town Moor, the dirty city's green lung. As a small child it was a major attraction having rows of lurid sideshows featuring all kinds of freaks and oddities, as well as naked women behind gauze sheets – 'nobody under sixteen allowed son', said the 'barker', but somehow we always managed to sneak in. Lots of unsavoury looking characters lolled around dozens of Gypsy caravans.

Being summer in England and also the school holidays, it was of course raining buckets, it never failed when the Hoppings came to town. There were wild rides such as the bone jarring dodgem cars and the vomit inducing waltzer. With wilder music, well, louder anyway, by artists like Dicky Valentine and Tommy Steele, both of whom Eric held in utter contempt as being inferior English imitations of American artists. Tommy Steele, in particular, received Eric's scorn because he took American chart hits and recorded an English cover version before the American original was released in the UK.

It was around mid-1962 as I remember, when The Animals started to coalesce as a group. They didn't coalesce as individuals however, still being far apart in personalities.

At first, I didn't reckon much for Chas Chandler's talent as a bass player, and he had completely different musical tastes from Eric, me and the rest of the band. Chas was more pop oriented, and he loved the early Beatles. I was wrong to think that Chas Chandler was lightest talent in the band, it's ironic he would go on in the music business to make probably more money than the rest of the band put together, managing Jimi Hendrix, Slade and other big groups.

The band continued to play music that was not on the radar of the mainstream pop fan in the UK, and fortunately for music history Eric's firm insistence and uncompromising personality kept it that way.

Alan Price was a constant challenge because his interest leaned more to bigger bands with a more extensive instrumental line up. Although there were big differences, in my opinion, Eric and Alan were the most exceptional members of the group that by some miracle had come together. Eric has always had an amazing voice and Alan was a truly brilliant keyboard player. Together, they had the potential to have been a great song writing team, but in personalities and tastes they remained poles apart.

"SPINAL TAP HAD NOTHING ON THE ANIMALS" KEITH ALTHAM

Alan could not sing to save his life, his voice was poor at that time. His singing obviously improved later, as proven by his own post-Animals releases and compositions.

Eric is a natural-born singer and he believes in the subjects he sings about, which is critical to his success I think, because the microphone can be a devastating revealer of insincerity. By far the most amicable guy in the band, who always had a 'Happy Jack' attitude, was drummer John Steel who music critic, Keith Altham once described as 'the most balanced drummer in the universe.' John is still touring today with a band called The Animals and Friends, pounding out the vintage original Animals' hits on the nostalgia circuit. I've seen some of their performances online, John sounds as good as ever but the lead singer is miles away from being able to deliver those hits with the same blistering force as Eric. The tunes are the recognisable old Animals' favourites, but without the distinctive voice of Eric Burdon, they just don't sound the same.

John is an accomplished drummer and the only member of the original band in The Animals and Friends. As for Hilton Valentine, I still believe his innovative opening of an 'A' minor arpeggiated chord guitar on *The House of The Rising Sun* never got the credit deserved. He was, and is, a great guitar player.

By my recollection, it is ironic that the member of the band who was most reluctant in putting *The House of The Rising Sun* together, Alan Price, was the only one to benefit financially in a substantial way. But you can't devalue Alan Price's keyboard playing, and he went on to an impressive musical career of his own, but it was Eric that found and modified the song's lyrics and Hilton Valentine's signature guitar playing that will never be forgotten. Perhaps Alan got the credit and the royalties but Eric Burdon personified The Animals.

It's not hard to understand why the remaining original Animals – Eric, John and Hilton still hold some resentment towards Alan Price. If only one credit was allowed on the recording, *The House of The Rising Sun* as the band had been told, it could easily have been 'Trad. Arr. The Animals' with everyone benefiting because it would be a combined creative effort. That single action changed the entire life and careers of Eric, John and Hilton, but as John Steel said of the time, 'We didn't know sh*t from clay, we just signed.'

If it had been credited as 'Trad. Arr. The Animals', Eric and John would not still be thrashing themselves today on tour. Touring with a band is tough, and not easy on the constitution of seventy-plus year olds. John might be enjoying a peaceful retirement with his lovely wife Ann, and Eric quietly contemplating the stars in the desert and working on his umpteenth project, recording or book. It did even more damage, it contributed to the end of what might have developed into a world-class group like The Stones or The Beatles. Alan Price always refused to discuss the matter and in fact refused to talk about why he refused to talk.

Now, this might be a bit of a stretch, but one of my favourite musicologists, Alan Lomax, said during his early research that the melodic timing and structure of *The House of the Rising Sun* is similar to the 16th century English ballad *Greensleeves* (written around 1580). It follows the ballad structure of four-line stanzas with a rhyme between the second and fourth lines, and is also a northern ditty about a prostitute. Did we go full circle here? To a Northern England lad making famous a distant iteration of the ballad about a brothel under the name of *The House of the Rising Sun* almost 400 years later?

There is a lot of conflicting information about the origin of The Animals' name and I have read at least a dozen different accounts. Anyone who saw the original Animals perform knows it was not derived from their

"WE DIDN'T KNOW SH*T FROM CLAY, WE JUST SIGNED" JOHN STEEL

wild stage performances as some have claimed; they were not in the least bit wild.

I remember the naming of the band this way. We were having a drink one day in The Crow's Nest on Percy Street in Newcastle near the Haymarket. There had been general discussion off and on about a new name for the group for several days, but everyone (except Alan of course) felt the band could not go forward being called The Alan Price Combo. The name was just not exciting or catchy and did not reflect where Eric wanted to go musically.

There is a back story to the final naming of the band. During one of our forays into the local countryside to get drunk, smash up country pubs, create general mayhem and sleep rough (Eric was probably taking revenge on the rural locals for misleading him about *The Archers* radio show when he was younger) we often hung out with a loosely organised local gang called The Squatters led by a character called 'Animal' Hogg. Eric took an instant liking to 'Animal' Hogg because he was ex-army and had the military bearing about him. Animal was a little unhinged due to his military experiences, but he and Eric became fast friends.

These forays got out of hand, degenerating into the destruction of pub toilets and punching out windows, they attracted the attention of the local press who described The Squatters gang as 'the scourge of the

Eric with the Alan Price Combo, Club A Go-Go.

(Jimmy Perry)

North East' and 'acting like Animals.' I remember my mother asked me at the time 'you're not one of those acting like bloody wild Animals I'm reading about in the *Chronicle* are you?'

Eric and I sat talking about the exploits of The Squatters in The Crow's Nest that day and he, with his particular affection for 'Animal' Hogg, who had recently drowned, thought the name of the band should be 'Animal Hogg and The Squatters' as a posthumous tribute to him and our motley crew. I agreed with him because after all, as he had pointed out, the local newspaper (*The Chronicle*) already called us animals as a derogatory term. It appealed to Eric's sense of perversity and justice to turn the insult into a payback by being proud of the tag. I don't remember Hilton or Chas being present at this particular meeting, but John Steel and Alan Price were, and they were not enthusiastic about that suggestion.

After much back and forth, including a discussion of the success of The Beatles' name, all present finally decided on the name 'The Animals.' So it was Eric who came up with the suggestion that led to the name of the group.

Alan Price didn't agree with the name one bit, he just couldn't see the appeal of a band of which he was a member, deriving its name from the sobriquet for such an uncouth character. But I think in his mind his main disagreement with the name of the band was it didn't include his name somewhere.

That is my recollection, I was there that day in The Crow's Nest and it's the way both Eric and I remember it. (It was particularly galling to Eric when several decades later in 2008, a British Court denied him the right to use the name).

Willingly or unwillingly, Eric has always carried The Animals' torch and to set the record straight about the start of Eric's career, he did not join the Alan Price Combo prior to that group becoming The Animals. The Pagans, Eric's original group coexisted with The Alan Price Combo. Eric also sometimes sang with them, as he often did with other groups in the very early days. Eventually, it was Alan Price who joined the Pagans (Eric's group), bringing the Alan Price Combo name, which was subsequently dropped to be replaced with The Animals.

Although all those present that day in The Crow's Nest were now in agreement with the new name for the group it had to be cemented by higher authorities like manager, Mike Jeffery and record companies, but the final and the most important endorsement for the name came from Ronan O'Rahilly, the Irish businessman who owned Radio Caroline the offshore 'pirate' radio station. Ronan O'Rahilly and Radio Caroline played an important part in helping all the British rock groups get a hearing

The Crow's Nest Pub, Haymarket, early 1960s. Scene of the meeting which originated The Animals' name.

(Dezo Hoffmann/Rex Shutterstock)

with the public because the government-controlled BBC would not play Rock & Roll music at the time. They even considered Tom Jones as inappropriate for general broadcasting. The BBC had a lock on radio and TV broadcasting and all the major record companies followed their guidelines and 'requirements' or their artists had no chance of getting any air time.

Operating outside British territorial waters Radio Caroline was the only place British teenagers could hear the new popular 'rock' music, apart from Radio Luxembourg. It was Radio Caroline that helped the likes of The Stones, The Who, The Kinks and The Animals to get their careers started. I know Eric is grateful to this day for the part Ronan O'Rahilly played in helping to make The Animals famous.

Ronan O'Rahilly probably did more to advance The Animals career than their manager Mike Jeffery ever did, and Ronan never got any credit. In fact one might go as far as to say the so called 'British Invasion' of the USA might never have happened, or at least happened much later, without Ronan O'Rahilly and Radio Caroline. The BBC gave up their silly policy after about five years when they saw that Radio Caroline and the other pirate radio stations were logging over twenty million British and European teenage listeners.

The Animals, now established by their first recordings, started touring and playing with their early idols like Chuck Berry, Carl Perkins and Jimmy Witherspoon. The sixties and the psychedelic excesses of that decade never really impacted on Newcastle upon Tyne. Our city was up in the north east corner of England where almost everyone was still struggling just to make a living. Anyway the weather precluded any outdoor 'hippy' gatherings because almost all of the time it was cold or wet, but clubs like the Downbeat and Club A Go-Go were jumping pockets of activity reflecting the new music and culture.

The sixties 'hippy' era had more impact in London where Eric and The Animals had now ensconced themselves. Even there though, it was not quite the swinging sixties as described by the press hype and was often impeded by the weather. I believe the general absence of street demonstrations and riots common in warmer climes don't happen as much in England, not because of the English conservative attitude but the bloody awful English weather. But it was in the sixties when we all began to feel truly more emancipated. Despite the grimy atmosphere and chilling cold and rain, miniskirts and 'go-go' boots flourished.

The Animals were the house band of Mike Jeffery's Club A Go-Go and it was only with the driving insistence of Eric that they decamped to London, later to became famous and take America by storm. Lots of fundamental changes were taking place in the sixties in the North East, although the Pill had not hit teenagers in Newcastle, because officially it was only available to married women. As for the place to go for Newcastle teenagers interested in the new Rock & Roll, the centre of the universe was now the Oxford Ballroom in New Bridge Street. The number of successful bands that emerged from the UK in the sixties was amazing, many of them being from the industrial North of England.

Newcastle always had a healthy share of 'hard men', these violent and unpredictable characters are part of the history of 'the Toon' and local organised crime. While he was on tour in the eighties, Eric had a run in with one of these individuals who insisted on being allowed into a closed rehearsal. After a brief confrontation, with the rest of the band cowering in the studio, Eric escaped with just a bloody nose. These were dangerous and unpredictable people and Eric knew it, but as always he stood his ground.

During The Animals' first American tour, Eric had sniffed the general ambiance of the USA and felt the proximity of things he had been passionate about all his life. He also found the dry climate in California beneficial for his asthma. He decided he would not settle back in the UK for the rest of his natural life.

"I HAVE THE RIGHT TO CALL MYSELF THE ANIMALS. I WAS THE LEAD SINGER IN THE BAND, IT WAS ME WHO CAME UP WITH THE NAME AND I'VE WORKED WITH IT FOR DECADES." ERIC BURDON

GONNA SEND YOU BACK TO WALKER

It was America that invented Eric Burdon and The Animals. Without America's rich heritage of blues and folk music inspiring them, rock music history might have been entirely different.

Eric, born in Walker, Newcastle now lives in Ojai, California. Hilton Valentine born in South Shields now lives in New Hampshire. John Steel, born in Gateshead, now lives in Longframlington, Northumberland. Alan Price born in Durham, now lives in Barnes near London. Chas Chandler, now deceased, was born in Heaton, Newcastle. I now live in Las Vegas.

Eric is still touring the US and Europe, and continues writing and recording music. John is touring Europe drumming away with The Animals and Friends. Alan Price emerges once a month to play at his local pub. Hilton is still writing and recording, and being Hilton, still loves skiffle. Chas is probably trying to get recording contracts for those aspiring musical souls between heaven and hell.

There have been negative comments about Eric's two previous autobiographies, mainly because he rarely mentions his creative process – writing music, recording, his inspiration and what makes him tick musically. I believe, after knowing him for so long, the reason he does not write much about the music making process is because to Eric, in a way, it is a means to an end. He is interested in so many forms of expression and experiences. 'I'm not quite sure what I do' he once said 'I'm not really a musician, I'm an instrument. That's what I say to my bands. Don't expect anything else, you guys have got to play me, you send the signals through me and I do what I do, I'm not quite sure myself what that is'.

Consider the number of bands, line ups and musical genres he has woven his creativity around for the last fifty years. I asked him about these comments and his answer was 'I prefer to write about the "living flesh" around music, I'm interested in the whole human experience.' I can understand where he is coming from.

I have been instrumental in the creation of some of the most exotic and fantastic casino buildings around the world all my professional life. If I were to write a book about my career it would not be about building the buildings, it would be about the fascinating, weird, cornucopia of odd and eccentric characters and situations encountered on each project. The actual buildings are my means to an end, it's the situations and human experiences, the 'living flesh' as Eric described it to me that is the most interesting. This is what Eric so ably does in his autobiographies. Eric was never dominated by his music; his chosen career is only a part of who he is.

Eric is a voracious reader and can discuss with you everything from the paranormal to quantum theory. We once had a discussion over a period of three days on 'Zero Point Energy and the Nazi Bell.' He loves writing and storytelling and of course today he is a completely different human being from decades ago, just as we all are.

Eric has always kept a huge journal of his writings and drawings from which he often extracts inspiration for his songs. Although he lost one of these extensive journals in a house fire, another he lent to Nina Simone, never to be returned. He still has a huge compendium of his writings, notes, sketches and ideas.

Andy Blackford said in his book *Wild Animals*, 'Eric is a restless spirit that could never retire to a cottage in Northumberland like drummer John Steel. He is possessed with a power and a passion, which will always conjure him up an audience, even when he's only firing on three cylinders.' In fact John never retired to a cottage; he has lived in the same cottage for decades which demonstrates again how far apart in personalities this band really were.

Recently, Eric was almost late for a gig at the Del Mar racetrack near San Diego, we got so involved in discussing a History Channel TV program in his hotel room we forgot to leave for the venue. We screeched up

"YOU WON'T AMOUNT TO A BLOODY THING LAD, YOU'RE JUST A WASTER."

to the backstage trailer with seconds to spare, Eric focusing on telling me about a movie that had been made at the race track, not the stage he is about to jump on. Another example of this relaxed attitude was when Eric called me fifteen minutes before he was due on stage at the El Cajon gig at the Sycuan Casino in California to discuss something about his new book. He has no backstage or pre-performance jitters at all. Backstage he can be deep in conversation or reading a book and when he is cued up he will close the book and like turning on a switch, immediately jump on stage and take off like a rocket.

Today, Eric has some concepts in mind which don't involve song writing or recording, these will probably be on the kitchen table again after he completes his international tour. I think one of these projects will surprise everyone. I know at some point Eric would like to write a novel, as he said: 'I've been living pure fiction so I might as well try writing some.'

It's now late October 2013 and Eric is about to leave the USA for approximately three months on an extensive tour of Europe, spending most of the time in Germany where he has a loyal and fervent fan base. After the tour it's likely he will direct his attention to more non-performance endeavours concerning things he feels passionately about. He still has a lot to say about the human experience that he is capable of expressing in a variety of forms.

Eric, the perennial rebel, has an acute sense of the social order of things and is a perceptive observer of the social and political scene. Who knows, Eric will always be Eric, defying the norm. As he told me, 'I always knew it would be a lifetime's work to achieve what I want to achieve for myself.'

Eric is a desert denizen through and through, so Ojai, with its more Mediterranean climate, has presented some challenges which he responds to in his own way. He has just acquired the 'Shark', as he calls it, a 1972 Chevy Impala convertible, not only for his love of the American car of the past but also, being Eric, to make a statement, careening around the narrow, hilly country roads of Ojai he shouts over the wind, 'I want people to remember Detroit – America used to make real cars, not the little computerised boxes on wheels made today.' I agree, as the once the proud owner of a 1972 Cadillac Eldorado convertible. Although, eight miles per gallon saw that beauty on its way.

Recently, after months of conflict with the Ojai City Council, coupled with threats of heavy fines, Eric decided to comply with the city's request to take down the three-panel fence in the front yard; this was erected to stop headlights flashing in the front window and disturbing his sleep. The fact he sleeps elsewhere in the house is irrelevant to our hero. 'I've got a bloody great hammer, I'll have it down in seconds' he told us. Marianna and I head for the fence with crowbars. After several minutes of struggling through bushes and trees we realise there is no sign of Eric or his hammer. 'Listen' said Marianna, 'he's never done that before, he never *ever* plays it.'

From the rear of the house came the strains of the Animals' original recording of *House of The Rising Sun*. Eric was floating leisurely in the swimming pool. He had been talking to me about going back to a simple combo instead of the current band and I think this was his moment of defiance.

A court ruling in November 2013 awarded Eric the rights once again to use The Animals' name with his own. John Steel had filed to capture The Animals' name rights because no one else had. But in 2013, eight years of litigation resulted in the earlier ruling being overturned in favour of Eric Burdon (decision 0-369-13 trade mark application #2355587). The court ruled that because none of the original members of the group objected to any one or more of the others participating in what could be called for want of a better expression 'heritage' groups, none of them ever abandoned their ights. The legal tussle began in 2005 when Eric opposed n attempt by John to register the group's name as his JK trademark to sell CDs and concert tickets.

Eric always said 'I have the right to call myself The Animals, I was the lead singer in the band, it was me who came up with the name and I've worked with it for decades, so I think I can call myself whatever I want.'

Eric argued he, not Steel, was the band's 'living personification.' His lawyer said: 'No one remembers the drummer.' This opinion was rejected by an adjudicator from the Government's Intellectual Property Office who ruled in John Steel's favour, adding: 'I trust she [Burdon's lawyer] does not encounter Ringo Starr!'

In my opinion, the bottom line to Eric Burdon's road from a blue collar childhood, poor education and a debilitating medical condition to world fame and induction into the 'Rock & Roll Hall of Fame' was that he never changed his goal, and he was always totally self-propelled. He never really needed a Mike Jeffery. He did a whole lot better than his great-great uncle Geordie Ridley, and he has stayed true to who he is. So even if you happen to be a jerk or people think you're a jerk, just stay true to who you are.

This story would not be complete without trying to draw a line under the pivotal points that affected Eric's multi-decade career and that in his mind remain unresolved. You might call them the three demons that still haunt him – Mike Jeffery, Alan Price and Jimi Hendrix.

Eric's first contact with Mike Jeffery was as a designer for Jeffrey's Club A Go-Go while Eric was still an art student and struggling with an embryonic band. As the band started to coalesce he saw Jeffery as a possible manager and mentioned it to Alan Price who concurred. Pleas from the band to Jeffery to manage them were ignored at first. Jeffery had no interest in music at all according to Eric, it was the money from his Newcastle clubs that interested him. As soon as the band began to make an impression however, he jumped on the management deal.

Jeffery met an untimely death in 1973 when the plane bringing him back from a trip to Majorca collided with another plane over Nantes in France. The accident occurred a few years after Jimi Hendrix died in London. Jeffery was on his way back to a court hearing in London concerning Hendrix when he died. His body was rumoured to have washed up on a French beach still wearing an expensive suit with a briefcase of money handcuffed to his wrist, floating in wads of cash. Jimi Hendrix's girlfriend of the time, Kathy Etchingham, has busted some of the myths that grew up around Jeffery's death saying that the plane crashed well inland from the sea, there was no floating money and victims of the crash could only be identified by their dental records.

To this day, Eric is both fascinated and repelled by Jeffery, knowing that the management of the Animals and their financial misadventure forced his life to take a completely different path.

At the time of the Animals' formation, Alan Price was still working as a clerk in the Newcastle tax office while moonlighting with other musicians. Alan was a loner in a close group and acted like it. Eric was certainly difficult to deal with at times, but Alan was just as difficult. He definitely was on another page, but Eric said it was worth putting up with just about anything because the man was amazing on the keyboard, 'a wizard', he said.

But Eric holds no animosity towards Price, recognising his brilliance as a musician, but still struggles with yet another relationship that changed the course of his career.

"YOU'RE NOT ONE OF THOSE ACTING LIKE BLOODY WILD ANIMALS I'M READING ABOUT IN THE CHRONICLE ARE YOU?"

THE DEATH OF JIMI HENDRIX

The official version of Hendrix's death states he was unable to sleep on the night of 17 September 1970, and took nine sleeping pills belonging to his 'girlfriend', Monica Danneman. Monica Danneman always claimed she was Jimi's girlfriend/fiancée, but according to people in a position to know – Eric and Jimi's actual girlfriend Kathy Etchingham, Monica was a brief and very late entry in Jimi's life. Jimi had no other love than his music and no time for establishing a serious relationship. Eric remembers Monica's relationship with Jimi only lasting a few days. The inspiration for *Foxy Lady* and *The Wind Cries Mary* is said to have been Kathy Etchingham.

Eric was the first person, other than Monica Danneman to be aware of the death of Jimi Hendrix. The first call she made was to Hendrix's good friend Eric Burdon. Eric told me he yelled at her on the phone to call an ambulance 'NOW!' Approximately three hours later she called Eric again saying she still couldn't wake Hendrix. This time Eric screamed at her and then rushed over to Jimi's apartment. When he arrived the ambulance had already taken Hendrix away.

Eric formed the opinion that Hendrix was deeply religious, he based this on a poem Hendrix had written on the day of his death. Eric found it on a crumpled piece of paper he picked up from the bedroom floor.

The poem title was *The Story of Life* which ended with the simple line 'the story of life is hello and goodbye until we meet again.'

A few days after Jimi Hendrix's death, Eric appeared on a television show in London and suggested Hendrix had committed suicide. Eric regrets this interview to this day telling me he was completely stoned. Eric blames this bizarre TV interview for messing up his career for years afterwards.

Eric remembers Jimi as a really nice guy, a brilliant guitarist and songwriter but at the end a man who had completely lost his way. The bottom line is that it still nags at Eric, going back through all the events unfolding at the time and wondering what he could have done differently.

Today, our rebellious rocker packs all these memories with him still as he once again prepares to hit the road singing the hits and living with his demons.

Here is where I thought this little story might end. However, after what was a successful European tour Eric is now back in Ojai and on the phone once more, within minutes he asks me to make another trip to see him. Apparently his new shoes have shrunk since last week and at 3am a watermelon exploded in the kitchen cupboard. Life was back to normal in Eric's World.

"ERIC WAS THE FIRST, APART FROM MONICA DANNEMAN TO BE AWARE OF THE DEMISE OF JIMI HENDRIX."

"M REALLY STILL A CHILD OF THE FORTIES. I STILL THINK ABOUT IT A LOT, ABOUT THE PERCUSSIONS OF ARMED CONFLICT. UNTIL 1953 WE HAD RATIONING. WE COULDN'T BUY MEAT, WE COULDN'T BUY PLEASURABLE GOODS LIKE CIGARETTES AND SWEETS."

C BURDON

na Burdon